Allegheny Portage Railroad National Historic Site and Johnstown Flood National Memorial

Weather of 2009

Natural Resource Data Series NPS/ERMN/NRDS—2010/081

Paul Knight, Tiffany Wisniewski, Chad Bahrmann, and Sonya Miller

Pennsylvania State Climate Office
503 Walker Building
Pennsylvania State University
University Park, Pennsylvania

September 2010

U.S. Department of the Interior
National Park Service
Natural Resource Program Center
Fort Collins, Colorado

The National Park Service, Natural Resource Program Center publishes a range of reports that address natural resource topics of interest and applicability to a broad audience in the National Park Service and others in natural resource management, including scientists, conservation and environmental constituencies, and the public.

The Natural Resource Data Series is intended for timely release of basic data sets and data summaries. Care has been taken to assure accuracy of raw data values, but a thorough analysis and interpretation of the data has not been completed. Consequently, the initial analyses of data in this report are provisional and subject to change.

All manuscripts in the series receive the appropriate level of peer review to ensure that the information is scientifically credible, technically accurate, appropriately written for the intended audience, and designed and published in a professional manner. This report received informal peer review by subject-matter experts who were not directly involved in the collection, analysis, or reporting of the data. Data in this report were collected and analyzed using methods based on established, peer-reviewed protocols and were analyzed and interpreted within the guidelines of the protocols.

Views, statements, findings, conclusions, recommendations, and data in this report do not necessarily reflect views and policies of the National Park Service, U.S. Department of the Interior. Mention of trade names or commercial products does not constitute endorsement or recommendation for use by the U.S. Government.

This report is available from the Eastern Rivers and Mountains Network (http://science.nature.nps.gov/im/units/ERMN) and the Natural Resource Publications Management website (http://www.nature.nps.gov/publications/NRPM).

Please cite this publication as:

Knight, P., T. Wisniewski, C. Bahrmann, and S. Miller. 2010. Allegheny Portage Railroad National Historic Site and Johnstown Flood National Memorial: Weather of 2009. Natural Resource Data Series NPS/ERMN/NRDS—2010/081. National Park Service, Fort Collins, Colorado.

NPS 423/105522, 439/105522, September 2010

Table of Contents

Figures

Tables

List of Key Acronyms

ALPO   Allegheny Portage Railroad National Historic Site

COOP   National Weather Service Cooperative Observer Program

CWOP   Citizen Weather Observer Program

ERMN   Eastern Rivers and Mountains Network

FAA   Federal Aviation Administration

GOES   Geostationary Operational Environmental Satellite

NHS   National Historic Site

IFLOWS   Integrated Flood Observing and Warning System

JOFL   Johnstown Flood National Memorial

NADP   National Atmospheric Deposition Program

NARR   North American Regional Reanalysis

NCDC   National Climatic Data Center

NOAA   National Oceanic and Atmospheric Administration

NMem   National Memorial

NWS   National Weather Service

PDSI   Palmer Drought Severity Index

POR   Period of Record

PRISM   Parameter-elevation Regressions on Independent Slopes Model

RAWS   Remote Automated Weather Stations

USDM   United States Drought Monitor

USGS   United States Geological Survey

Introduction

Weather and climate are widely recognized as key drivers of terrestrial and aquatic ecosystems, affecting biotic as well as abiotic ecosystem characteristics and processes. Global and regional scale climatic patterns, trends, and variations are critical to the cycling of elements, nutrients, and minerals through the ecosystems and can deliver pollutants from regional and even global sources (National Assessment Synthesis Team 2001). These variations and trends influence the fundamental properties of ecologic systems such as soil-water relationships and plant-soil processes and their disturbance rates and intensity. Information obtained from meteorological monitoring will be useful to interpreting and understanding changes in species composition, community structure, water and soil chemistry, and related landscape processes (Marshall and Piekielek 2007).

The purpose of this report is to provide a concise weather and climate summary for the period from January 1 through December 31, 2009, and to place current patterns and trends in an appropriate historical and regional context (Knight et al., in preparation). It is our intention that this report will satisfy an inherent interest in meteorological phenomena and meets a portion of the Eastern Rivers and Mountains Network (ERMN) Weather and Climate Monitoring objectives:

- Document long-term trends in weather and climate through seasonal and annual summaries of selected parameters (e.g., multiple forms of precipitation, temperature).
- Identify and document extremes and averages of climatic conditions for common parameters (e.g., precipitation, air temperature) and other parameters where sufficient data are available (e.g., wind speed and direction, solar radiation).
- Provide information on near real-time weather parameters, historical climate patterns, and climate station metadata from a single, easy-to-use Internet portal.

To accomplish these objectives, a variety of atmospheric data streams were evaluated for their quality, longevity, and applicability to the ERMN parks. Since no single weather observing network contains all the pertinent measures of atmospheric phenomena to assess ecosystem health, an objective analysis of the data networks was developed and outlined in the Weather and Climate Monitoring Protocol for the Eastern Rivers and Mountains Network and Mid-Atlantic Network of the National Park Service (Knight et al., in preparation). Through this analysis, a select number of weather/climate observing stations were chosen as representative of each park and these are the primary data sources used to profile climate summary and trends.

In addition to a suite of summary tables, graphs, and narratives, we specifically identify a series of key climatological indicators to report status and trends on an annual basis and periodically in separate and more thorough reports. These key indicators are further described in the protocol (Knight et al., in preparation) and summarized in the body of this report.

1

The Climate of the of the South Central Mountains

Allegheny Portage Railroad National Historic Site (NHS) and Johnstown Flood National Memorial (NMem) are located in Pennsylvania Climate Division 8, also known as the South Central Mountains. A climate division is a region that is reasonably homogenous with respect to climatic and hydrologic characteristics and is frequently used for compiling climate statistics (http://www.esrl.noaa.gov/psd/data/usclimate/map.html). Pennsylvania is divided into 10 climate divisions.

The South Central Mountain region is generally considered to have a humid continental type of climate, but the elevated terrain and rolling mountains keep temperatures lower than surrounding areas. The prevailing westerly winds carry most of the weather disturbances that affect the region from the interior of the continent, with the Atlantic Ocean having only an occasional influence on the climate of the area (Davey et al. 2006). Coastal storms do, at times, affect the day-to-day weather, especially in the winter, though the air circulating southeastward from the Great Lakes dominates in the winter. Seldom do storms of tropical origin have an effect in this part of Pennsylvania, but the rough terrain has led to memorable severe floods in the warm half of the year (Gelber 2002).

Temperatures are moderately continental, with the tempering effects of the Great Lakes contributing to cloud production in the winter and mountain-valley circulation induced clouds reducing the heat during the summer. The lowest readings in the winter occur with polar air masses of Canadian origin settling over the Northeast after a fresh snowfall. The highest readings of the summer happen when the sub-tropical fair weather system, the Bermuda high, pushes westward into the Carolinas. Its clockwise circulation will direct hot, humid air from the Gulf region into the Laurel Highlands. Allegheny Portage Railroad National Historic Site tends to have greater daytime temperatures than Johnstown Flood National Memorial; however, Johnstown Flood National Memorial tends to have fewer sub freezing nights than the Allegheny Portage Railroad National Historic Site. The last freeze for the region typically occurs in May and the first frosts appear in late September or October.

Precipitation is fairly evenly distributed throughout the year. Annual amounts generally range between 36–54 in (914–1,371 mm), while the majority of places receive 40–46 in (1,016–1,168 mm). Greatest amounts usually occur in the spring and summer months, while February is the driest month, having about 2 in (51 mm) less than the wettest months. Precipitation tends to be somewhat greater in the higher terrain due to uplift and additional moisture from the Great Lakes. Based upon long-term averages, annual precipitation amounts tend to be greater at Allegheny Portage Railroad National Historic Site than at Johnstown Flood National Memorial.

Surface winds blow from the west and northwest in the cold season and from the southwest during the warm half of the year. Thunderstorms follow a frequency that matches the solar cycle between the equinoxes and reaches a peak near the summer solstice. Hail is relatively infrequent, but flash floods and damaging thunderstorm winds affect parts of the region each summer. On average, tornadoes pass through the area about once every two years. Ice storms, which can cause significant disruption, occur at irregular intervals and are primarily confined to the months between December and March (Kocin and Uccellini 2004).

Observing Stations

A total of eight weather observing stations, comprised of five observing networks, were selected around Allegheny Portage Railroad NHS and Johnstown Flood National Memorial. Representative stations within a 100-km range of each park were chosen based on several criteria, including proximity to the park, representativeness of the station to the park elevation profile, type and frequency of observations, the period of record of the data, and data availability (Knight et al., in preparation). A subset of these observing networks (IFLOWS, GOES, NADP, and CWOP; three total stations) are not yet utilized for these reports due to limited data availability and/or lack of data quality assurance (Bureau of Land Management 1997). Moreover, the percentage of time a station reports particular parameters (e.g., temperature) can influence its data inclusion. No stations were excluded in 2009 based on this criterion; therefore, a total of five stations were used for this report (Figure 1, Table 1).

In addition to the summary information available in this report, a near real-time data stream has been made available to the ERMN through a Web interface for the selected stations along with monthly, seasonal, and annual summaries. The Web interface is accessible through the following link: http://climate.met.psu.edu/gmaps/NPS_DEVELOPMENT/interface.php.

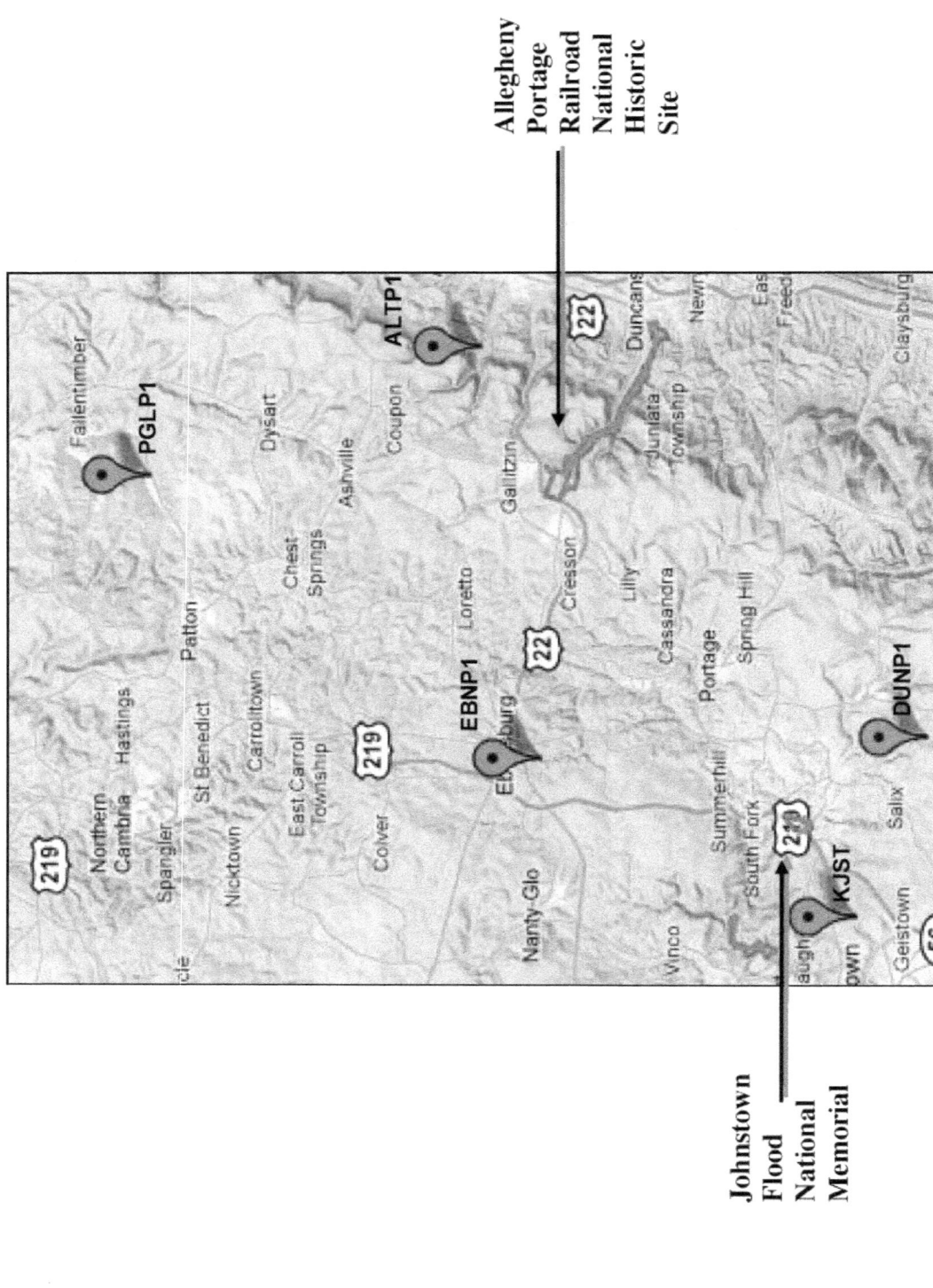

Figure 1. Location of weather observing stations around Allegheny Portage Railroad National Historic Site and Johnstown Flood National Memorial.

Table 1. List of weather observing stations around Allegheny Portage Railroad National Historic Site and Johnstown Flood National Memorial selected as best representative of the parks in 2009.

Station	Observing Network	Station Name	Period of Record (POR)		Percentage of Time Reporting Temperature for 2009	Percentage of Time Reporting Precipitation for 2009	Percentage of Time Reporting Temperature for entire POR	Percentage of Time Reporting Precipitation for entire POR
KJST	FAA	Johnstown	01/01/1973	Present	100.0	100.0	99.7	60.0
ALTP1	COOP	Altoona	10/01/1967	Present	100.0	100.0	95.6	96.0
EBNP1	COOP	Ebensburg Sewage Plant	02/01/1964	Present	100.0	100.0	99.4	99.4
PGLP1	COOP	Prince Gallitzin State Park	09/01/1982	Present	100.0	99.7	94.3	95.6
DUNP1	COOP	Dunlo	02/01/1992	Present	-	100.0	-	93.7

Temperature Summary

Calendar year 2009 was cooler than average for the Allegheny Portage Railroad National Historic Site and Johnstown Flood National Memorial region, with maximum temperatures averaging between 1–2 degrees Fahrenheit (°F) (0.6–1.2 degrees Celsius [°C]) below normal, though minimums were closer to normal values (Figures 2 and 3, Table 2). The maps in Figures 2 and 3 were created using estimates from the Parameter-elevation Regressions on Independent Slopes Model (PRISM). PRISM uses an interpolation scheme for temperature between actual observations and corrects these estimates for changes in topography across the region (Daly et al. 2002). More information can be found at http://www.prism.oregonstate.edu/.

January was quite cold, with readings more than 5°F (3.5°C) below average for Altoona, Ebensburg, Prince Gallitzin, and Johnstown, PA (Tables 3 and 4). The lowest readings of the year occurred in the middle of the month (January 17) as temperatures dropped as low as -20°F (-28.5°C) in the Laurel Highlands (Table 2). Temperatures in February were above normal with nighttime lows dipping to near 0°F (-17.8°C) on only one occasion. Positive temperature anomalies persisted into March as readings averaged as much as 2°F (1.2°C) above normal (Table 4). The winter months of January–February–March were the 43rd coolest in the South Central Mountain Climate Division of Pennsylvania since records began in 1895 (Table 5).

Spring began with above-normal daytime temperatures in April (Table 4). The average temperature in Ebensburg, PA, during the month was 48.4°F (9.1°C); 1.6°F (0.9°C) above average (Tables 3 and 4). Cool anomalies returned in May, though readings averaged just slightly below normal (between 0.9 and -1.1°F [0.5 and -0.6°C]; Table 4). The last 32°F (0°C) reading of the spring occurred on May 18 (Table 2). Very warm weather returned when five consecutive days at the end of June (22–26) saw high temperatures above 80°F (26.7°C). In its entirety, temperatures in the spring were the 25th warmest (Table 5).

The summer months of July–August–September were the 15th coolest since records began in 1895, in large part due to one of the coldest July's on record (Table 5). Warmer-than-normal readings occurred in August (Tables 3 and 4), but temperatures were slightly below average by September (Figures 2 and 3). The average temperature in July was 64.7°F (18.2°C) in Ebensburg, PA; 3.7°F (2.0°C) below average (Tables 3 and 4). Above-average temperatures returned in August with an average +0.5°F (0.3°C) temperature anomaly for the four stations. The highest temperature of the year occurred August 10 in Ebensburg, PA, with a reading of 89.0°F (31.9°C) (Table 2).

It was very cool during October as readings averaged between -2.2 to -3.8°F (-1.2 to 1.7°C) below the long-term mean (Table 4). The first 32°F (0°C) reading occurred on October 14, which is a little later than previous years. November brought a complete reversal with the largest positive anomalies of the year; Ebensburg averaged 43.6°F (6.4°C), which is 3.7°F (2.0°C) above normal (Table 4). Below-average temperatures occurred in December, which was -3.3°F (-1.8°C) below normal in Johnstown, PA (Table 4). Interestingly, 2009 featured a near-normal frequency of sub-freezing nights (Table 2), but above-normal number of cold days and well-below-normal number of hot days. The total growing season length (days between last spring freeze and first fall freeze) ranged from 140–181 days in 2009 (Table 2).

Allegheny Portage Railroad National Historic Site
and Johnstown Flood National Memorial
Departure from Average Monthly Maximum Temperature
2009 vs. 1971–2000

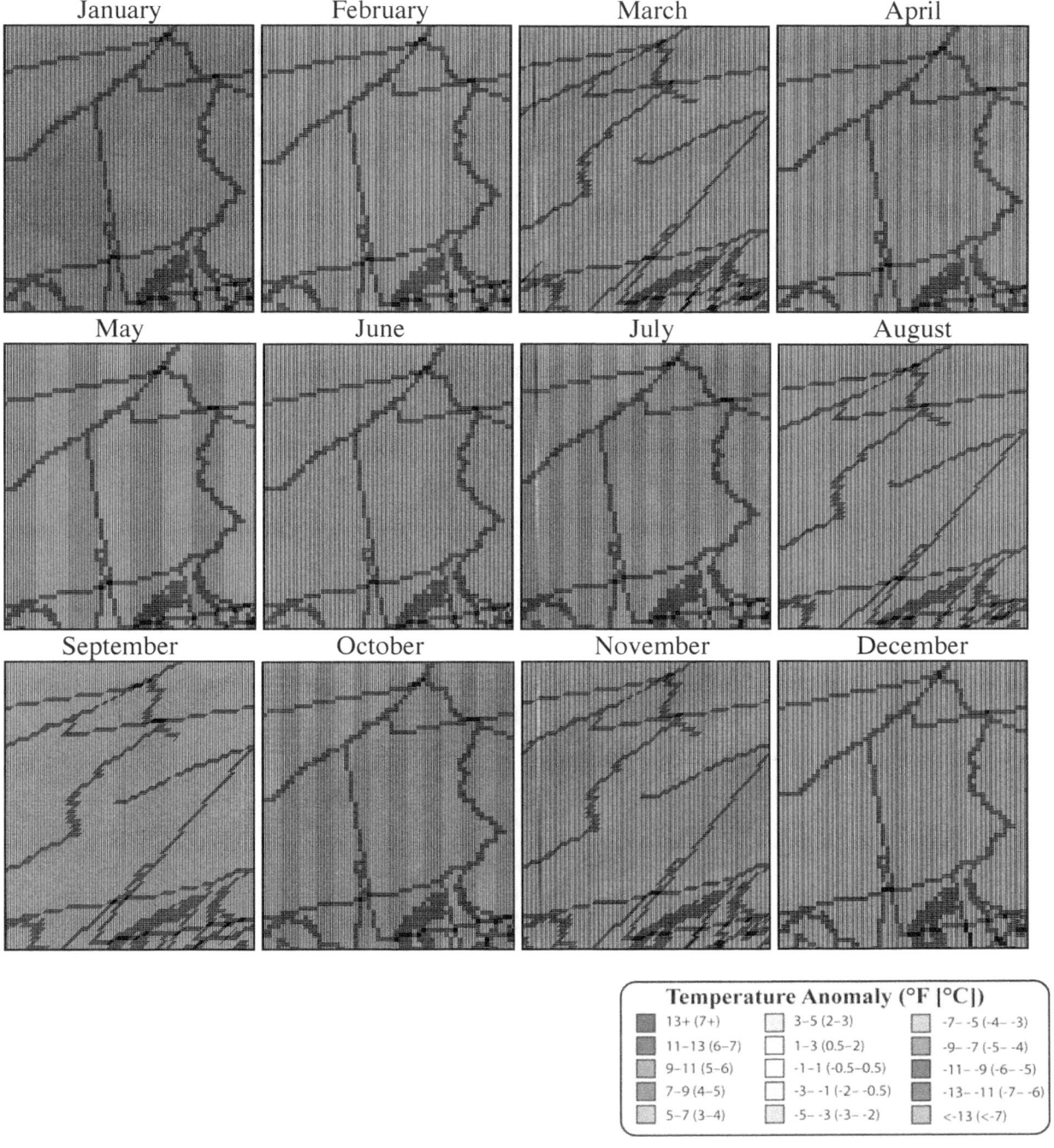

Figure 2. Maps showing departure from average monthly maximum temperature compared to the 30-year normal (1971–2000).

Allegheny Portage Railroad National Historic Site
and Johnstown Flood National Memorial
Departure from Average Monthly Minimum Temperature
2009 vs. 1971–2000

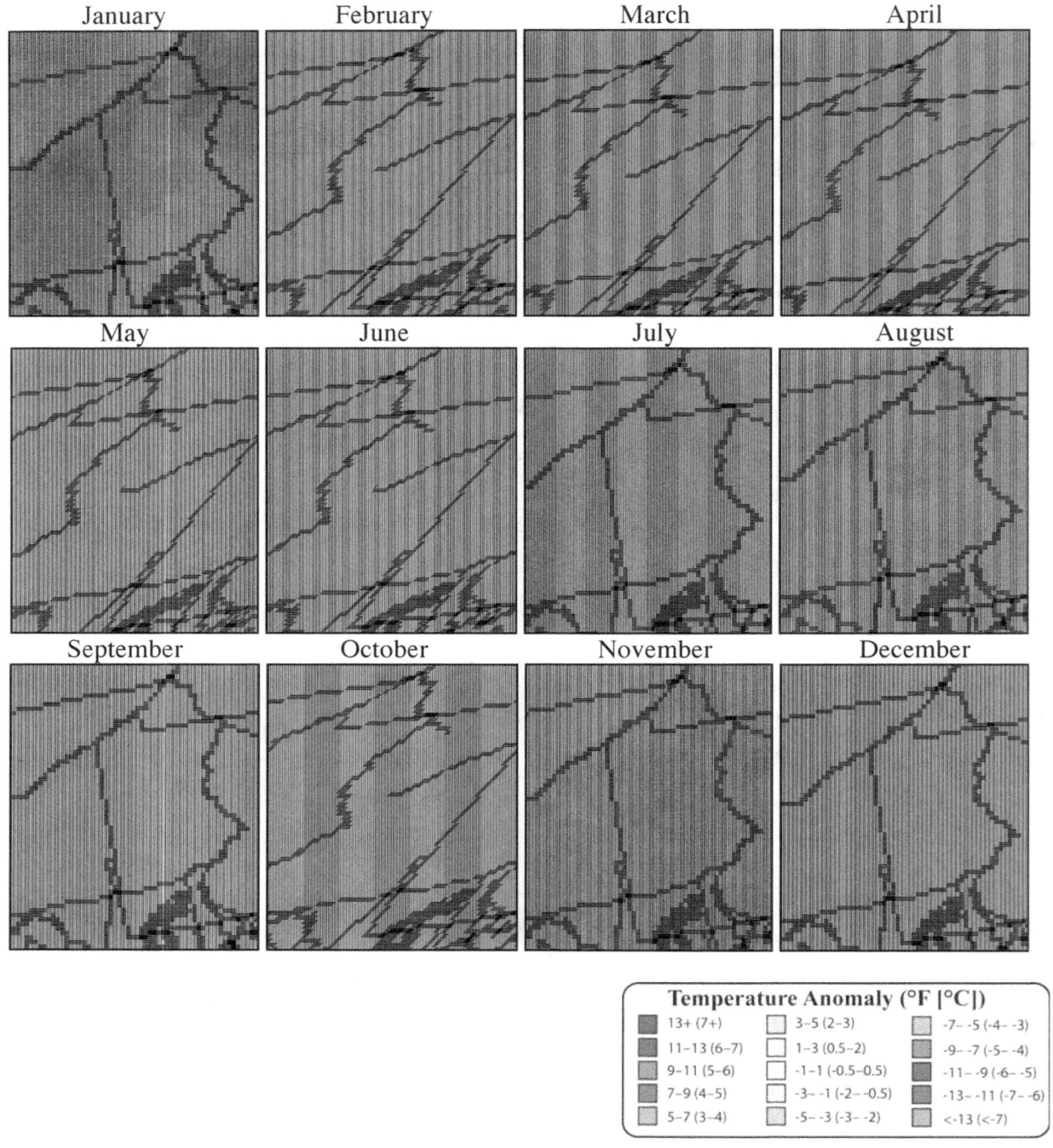

Figure 3. Maps showing departure from average monthly minimum temperature compared to the 30-year normal (1971–2000).

8

Table 2. Status of 2009 temperature indicators compared to the 30-year normal (1971–2000) at the Ebensburg (EBNP1) and Johnstown (KJST) stations.

Temperature Indicator	Ebensburg, PA 2009	Ebensburg, PA 1971–2000	Johnstown, PA 2009	Johnstown, PA 1971–2000
Average Annual Temperature	47.5°F 8.6°C	47.8°F 8.8°C	46.9°F 8.3°C	48.1°F 8.9°C
Average Annual Maximum Temperature	57.9°F 14.4°C	59.7°F 15.4°C	54.3°F 12.4°C	55.3°F 12.9°C
Summer Maximum (highest temperature)	89.0°F 31.7°C	90.1°F 32.3°C	85.0°F 29.4°C	91.1°F 32.8°C
Hot Days (days with Tmax≥90°F/32°C)	0	3	0	3
Average Annual Minimum Temperature	37.2°F 2.9°C	35.8°F 2.1°C	39.8°F 4.3°C	40.9°F 4.9°C
Winter Minimum (lowest temperature)	-20.0°F -28.9°C	-13.7°F -25.4°C	-7.6°F -22.0°C	-5.4°F -20.8°C
Cold Days (days with Tmax≤32°F/0°F)	38	35	57	53
Sub-freezing Nights (days with Tmin≤32°F/0°C)	139	161	128	125
Cold Winter Nights (days with Tmin≤0°F/-17.8°C)	5	10	3	4
Growing Season Length (days between last spring 32°F/0°C and first fall 32°F/0°C)	140	123	181	164

Table 3. Summary of monthly average temperatures for 2009 for the selected stations.

Station name	Station	Jan	Feb	Mar	Apr	May	Jun	Jul	Aug	Sep	Oct	Nov	Dec	Annual
Altoona, PA	ALTP1	20.4°F -6.4°C	29.9°F -1.2°C	38.6°F 3.7°C	49.2°F 9.6°C	58.2°F 14.6°C	65.7°F 18.7°C	67.0°F 19.4°C	70.4°F 21.3°C	61.6°F 16.4°C	48.9°F 9.4°C	44.7°F 7.1°C	28.0°F -2.2°C	48.6°F 9.2°C
Ebensburg, PA	EBNP1	20.1°F -6.6	29.6°F -1.3°C	38.8°F 3.8°C	48.4°F 9.1°C	57.4°F 14.1°C	64.0°F 17.8°C	64.7°F 18.2°C	68.2°F 20.1°C	60.1°F 15.6°C	47.8°F 8.8°C	43.6°F 6.4°C	27.2°F -2.7°C	47.5°F 8.6°C
Prince Gallitzin, PA	PGLP1	19.0°F -7.2	27.7°F -2.4°C	36.4°F 2.4°C	46.1°F 7.8°C	56.5°F 13.6°C	63.3°F 17.4°C	64.7°F 18.2°C	68.5°F 20.3°C	59.6°F 15.3°C	45.8°F 7.7°C	42.7°F 5.9°C	25.7°F -3.5°C	46.3°F 8.0°C
Johnstown, PA	KJST	18.9°F -7.3	28.3°F -2.1°C	37.5°F 3.1°C	47.7°F 8.7°C	57.1°F 13.9°C	63.9°F 17.7°C	64.9°F 18.3°C	67.6°F 19.8°C	59.3°F 15.2°C	47.3°F 8.5°C	43.4°F 6.3°C	26.4°F -3.1°C	46.9°F 8.3°C

Table 4. Summary of 2009 departure from normal temperature based on 30-year normal (1971–2000) for the selected stations.

Station name	Station	Jan	Feb	Mar	Apr	May	Jun	Jul	Aug	Sep	Oct	Nov	Dec	Annual
Altoona, PA	ALTP1	6.1°F	0.8°F	1.1°F	0.3°F	-0.8°F	-1.5°F	-4.1°F	0.6°F	-1.7°F	-3.0°F	2.6°F	-3.5°F	-1.3°F
		-3.3°C	0.4°C	0.7°C	0.2°C	-0.4°C	-0.9°C	-2.3°C	0.3°C	-1.0°C	-1.7°C	1.5°C	-1.9°C	-0.7°C
Ebensburg, PA	EBNP1	-5.2°F	1.9°F	2.2°F	1.6°F	0.9°F	-0.4°F	-3.7°F	1.0°F	-0.8°F	-2.2°F	3.7°F	-2.7°F	-0.4°F
		-2.9°C	1.1°C	1.2°C	0.9°C	0.5°C	-0.2°C	-2.0°C	0.5°C	-0.5°C	-1.2°C	2.0°C	-1.5°C	-0.2°C
Prince Gallitzin, PA	PGLP1	-5.4°F	0.6°F	0.7°F	-0.8°F	-0.8°F	-2.3°F	-5.1°F	0.4°F	-1.3°F	-3.8°F	2.7°F	-4.3°F	-1.6°F
		-3.0°C	0.3°C	0.3°C	-0.5°C	-0.5°C	-1.3°C	-2.8°C	0.2°C	-0.8°C	-2.1°C	1.5°C	-2.4°C	-0.9°C
Johnstown, PA	KJST	-6.2°F	-0.6°F	0.3°F	-0.8°F	-1.1°F	-2.1°F	-4.4°F	-0.6°F	-1.5°F	-2.3°F	3.5°F	-3.3°F	-1.3°F
		-3.0°C	-0.3°C	0.2°C	-0.5°C	-0.6°C	-1.2°C	-2.3°C	-0.4°C	-0.9°C	-1.2°C	2.0°C	-1.8°C	-0.7°C

*Indicates a station's period of record is less than 30 years. In these cases, the departure from normal values were calculated with normals derived from data spanning the length of the station's period of record.

Table 5. Seasonal temperature and precipitation rankings over 115 years (1 = warmest/wettest year and 115 = coldest/driest year) for Pennsylvania Climate Division 8.

PA Climate Division 8 Rankings "South Central Mountains"	Jan–Feb–Mar WINTER	Apr–May–Jun SPRING	Jul–Aug–Sep SUMMER	Oct–Nov–Dec AUTUMN
Temperature-2009	72	91	100	64
Precipitation-2009	114	36	75	13

Precipitation Summary

Liquid precipitation (rain and melted snow, ice, sleet, etc.; hereafter precipitation) was considerably below normal in 2009 around Johnstown Flood National Monument and Allegheny Portage Railroad National Historic Site (Table 6) with several notable dry spells (Table 7). The consistently negative precipitation anomalies allowed the year to rank as the 53rd driest in the South Central Mountain Climate Division (8) of Pennsylvania since records began in 1895.

The beginning of the year featured well-below-normal precipitation from January through April (Figure 4). In fact, the first three months of 2009 were the 2nd driest such period in 115 years of recordkeeping (Table 5). Between 8 and 10 in (200–260 mm) was tallied by the end of April (Tables 8 and 9); only 65% of normal. The start-of-the-year deficit began to be erased in May when 5.2 in (132 mm) of precipitation fell in the climate division. This was the 19th wettest May since records began in 1895. Snowfall, while below the long-term mean (Table 6), was abundant during January. At Johnstown, more than 23 in (60 cm) fell from January 14–31, 2009. Another 6 in (13 cm) was measured from February 20–24.

Spring was considerably more moist across the region, ranking as 36th wettest in the South Central Mountain Climate Division with 115 years of records (Table 5). The first week of May provided the region with 2–2.5 in (52–65 mm) of rain, ending a long dry period. The wettest location was Prince Gallitzin during June when 5.3 in (135 mm) was measured (Table 8). Only Ebensburg averaged slightly below-normal rainfall during the spring (Table 9).

The summer of 2009 had drier conditions return and ranked the 40th driest summer (Table 5), which oddly is almost exactly the same as in 2008. Both August and September saw negative precipitation anomalies with 81 and 69 percent of normal precipitation, respectively, in Johnstown, PA (Table 9). September was the driest in several years and ranked the 41st driest on record. The below-average precipitation was accompanied by the longest dry spell of the year, which occurred from August 30–September 6 (Table 7). There were no direct or indirect influences from tropical storms during this year.

Precipitation anomalies in the fall varied dramatically. October and December were both well above normal, ranking 8th and 5th wettest, respectively (Figure 3). Meanwhile, November was very dry, ranking the 20th driest. Despite the dry weather in November, the season concluded as the 13th wettest (Table 5). Three of the wettest days of the year occurred from late November into December (Table 7). As a whole, 2009 averaged around 6 in (155 mm) below the long-term mean and there were no extreme rainfall events during this year (Table 6).

Allegheny Portage Railroad National Historic Site
and Johnstown Flood National Memorial
Percent of Average Monthly Precipitation
2009 vs. 1971–2000

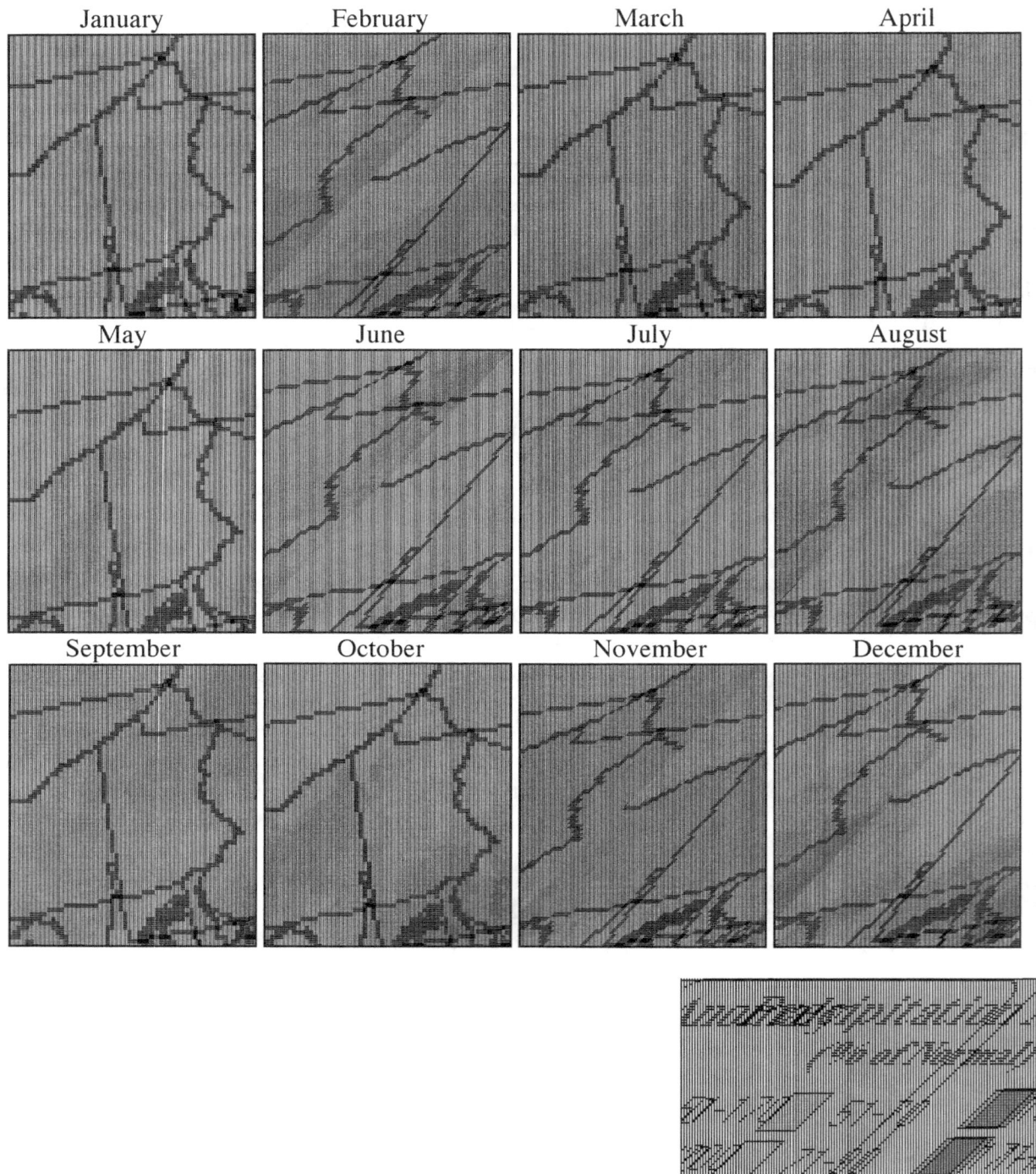

Figure 4. Maps showing percent of average monthly precipitation compared to the 30-year normal (1971–2000).

Table 6. Status of 2009 precipitation indicators compared to the 30-year normal (1971–2000) at the Ebensburg (EBNP1) and Johnstown (KJST) stations.

Precipitation Indicator	Ebensburg, PA 2009	Ebensburg, PA 1971-2000	Johnstown, PA 2009	Johnstown, PA 1971-2000
Annual Precipitation	43.4 in 1,102 mm	49.7 in 1,262 mm	33.5 in 851 mm	38.6 in 980 mm
Autumn (Oct, Nov, Dec) Precipitation	11.3 in 287 mm	11.1 in 282 mm	9.4 in 239 mm	8.8 in 224 mm
Heavy Rain (days with ≥1.0 in [25 mm] rain)	7	9	3	7
Extreme Rain (days with ≥2.0 in [51 mm] rain)	0	1	0	1
Micro-drought (strings of 7+ days without rain)	4	5	6	5
Annual Snowfall	72.5 in 1,842 mm	96.8 in 2,459 mm	67.0 in 1,702 mm	73.8 in 1,875 mm
Snow (days with ≥0.1 in [0.3 cm] snow)	37	45	43	38
Moderate Snow (days with ≥2.0 in [5.0 cm] snow)	20	21	15	14
Heavy Snow (days with ≥5.0 in [12.7 cm] snow)	1	3	2	3

Table 7. Top five wettest days and top five dry spells (consecutive days with a trace or less of rainfall) during 2009 from stations Ebensburg (EBNP1) and Johnstown (KJST).

Wettest Days in 2009	Dry Spells in 2009
Aug. 29: 1.8 in (46 mm)	Nov. 6–18
Jul. 22: 1.5 in (38 mm)	May 18–26
Nov. 20: 1.5 in (38 mm)	Feb. 28–Mar. 7
Dec. 9: 1.3 in (33 mm)	Aug. 30–Sept. 6
Nov. 19: 1.2 in (30 mm)	Jul. 4–10

Table 8. Summary of 2009 monthly total precipitation for selected stations.

Station name	Station	Jan	Feb	Mar	Apr	May	Jun	Jul	Aug	Sep	Oct	Nov	Dec	Annual
Johnstown, PA	KJST	1.9 in	1.3 in	1.3 in	2.6 in	4.7 in	2.7 in	4.3 in	3.0 in	2.6 in	4.0 in	1.8 in	3.3 in	33.5 in
		48 mm	33 mm	33 mm	66 mm	119 mm	69 mm	117 mm	76 mm	66 mm	102 mm	46 mm	84 mm	851 mm
Altoona, PA	ALTP1	2.7 in	1.3 in	1.6 in	4.0 in	4.8 in	4.6 in	4.2 in	2.1 in	2.7 in	5.8 in	2.4 in	5.7 in	41.9 in
		69 mm	33 mm	41 mm	102 mm	122 mm	117 mm	107 mm	53 mm	69 mm	147 mm	61 mm	145 mm	1,064 mm
Ebensburg, PA	EBNP1	3.7 in	2.2 in	1.7 in	3.0 in	4.6 in	4.1 in	5.7 in	4.3 in	2.9 in	4.0 in	2.6 in	4.8 in	43.6 in
		94 mm	56 mm	43 mm	76 mm	117 mm	104 mm	145 mm	109 mm	74 mm	102 mm	66 mm	122 mm	1,107 mm
Prince Gallitzin, PA	PGLP1	2.5 in	1.5 in	1.6 in	2.5 in	2.9 in	5.3 in	3.9 in	4.1 in	2.5 in	4.2 in	1.8 in	4.3 in	37.1 in
		64 mm	38 mm	41 mm	64 mm	74 mm	135 mm	99 mm	104 mm	64 mm	107 mm	46 mm	109 mm	942 mm
Dunlo, PA	DUNP1	2.6 in	1.9 in	1.2 in	2.9 in	4.3 in	2.9 in	4.3 in	4.2 in	2.4 in	4.7 in	1.2 in	3.9 in	36.5 in
		66 mm	48 mm	31 mm	74 mm	109 mm	74 mm	109 mm	107 mm	61 mm	119 mm	31 mm	99 mm	927 mm

Table 9. Summary of 2009 percent of normal precipitation based on 30-year normal (1971–2000) for selected stations.

Station name	Station	Jan	Feb	Mar	Apr	May	Jun	Jul	Aug	Sep	Oct	Nov	Dec	Annual
Johnstown, PA	KJST	79	56	38	73	123	83	115	81	69	160	48	137	89
Altoona, PA	ALTP1	97	50	44	109	109	108	104	65	67	172	66	195	99
Ebensburg, PA	EBNP1	95	68	39	69	97	92	114	107	67	118	63	128	88
Prince Gallitzin, PA	PGLP1	106	63	47	76	78	148	101	112	64	161	55	178	99
Dunlo, PA	DUNP1	76	79	32	71	104	67	122	101	54	154	33	139	86

*Indicates a station's period of record is less than 30 years. In these cases, the departure from normal values were calculated with normals derived from data spanning the length of the station's period of record.

14

Drought Status

There are a number of drought indices used to estimate the severity of drought in an area using algorithms that incorporate recent temperatures, rainfall, soil moisture, and other information (http://www.drought.gov). The main indices we report are the Palmer Drought Severity Index (PDSI) and the United States Drought Monitor (DM) – Drought Intensity Index. While both indices provides excellent summary information on broad-scale conditions, local conditions (such as at the park scale) may vary.

The PDSI is a soil moisture algorithm calibrated for relatively homogeneous regions and is calculated on a monthly basis using precipitation and temperature data, as well as the water content of the soil. The values vary between extremely moist (>4.0) and extreme drought (<-4.0) with "normal" values ranging between -1.9 and 1.9. Monthly PDSI values for Pennsylvania Climate Division 8 in 2009 are shown in Figure 5.

The DM – Drought Intensity Index is a synthesis of multiple indices (including the PDSI) and impacts and represents a consensus of federal and academic scientists. The DM produces a summary map of drought intensity for the nation and all states each week. It is on a scale ranging from abnormally dry (D0) to exceptional drought (D4). Mid-month (i.e., the second or third week) values for Pennsylvania (Figure 6) and the Northeast (Figure 7) are shown for 2009.

According to the PDSI, the dry weather during the winter in Climate Division 8 brought drought severity index values to a yearly minima in late April at a value less than 1.5. This value is still in the "normal" range and, moreover, regular rainfall starting in May brought the drought index back to positive ("moist") levels for much of the remainder of 2009. Dry conditions during September and November reduced the PDSI, but there was no widespread drought noted in the Allegheny Highlands (Figure 5). When comparing 2009 with previous years, the trend was nearly a mirror image of 2008 when dry weather began in June and continued into November. It is interesting to note that December, during the past three years, has been wetter than average. The DM – Drought Severity Index for Pennsylvania (Figure 6) and the Northeast (Figure 7) shows a similar pattern for the growing season (May through October); abnormally dry (D0) only during the beginning of May.

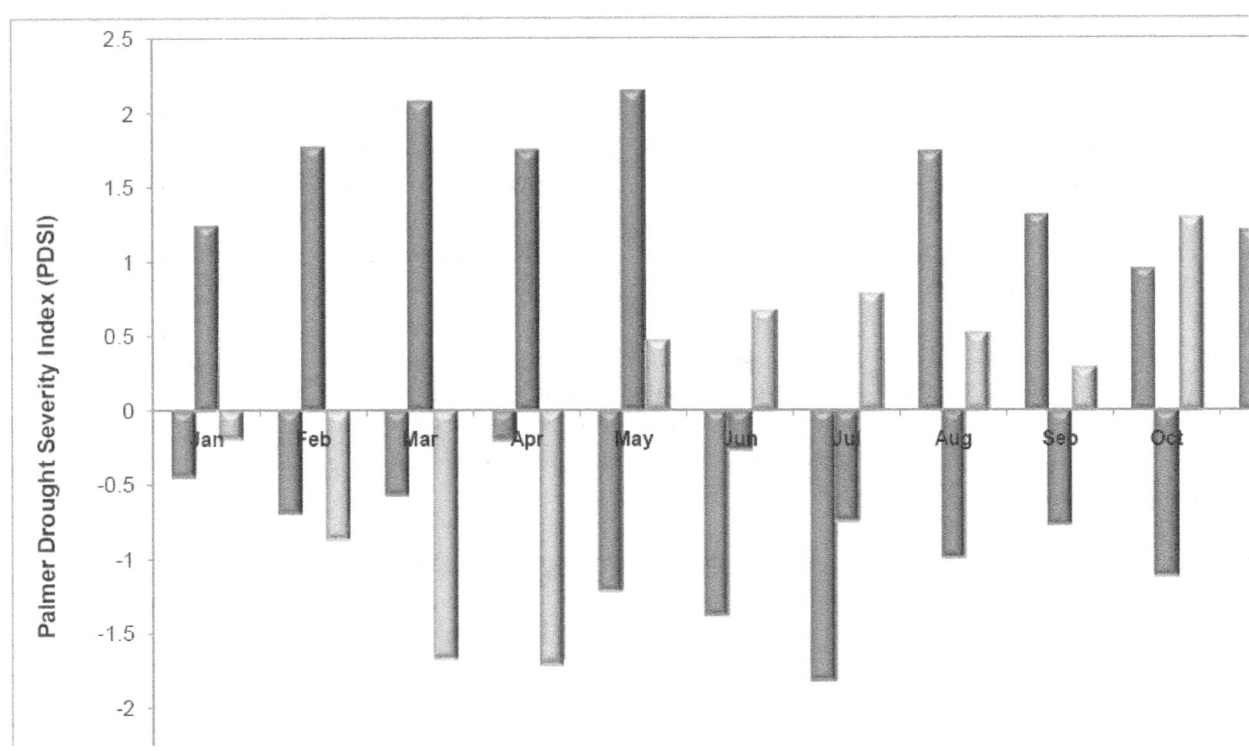

Figure 5. Monthly Palmer Drought Severity Index (PDSI) values for Pennsylvania Climate Division 8, 2007–2009.

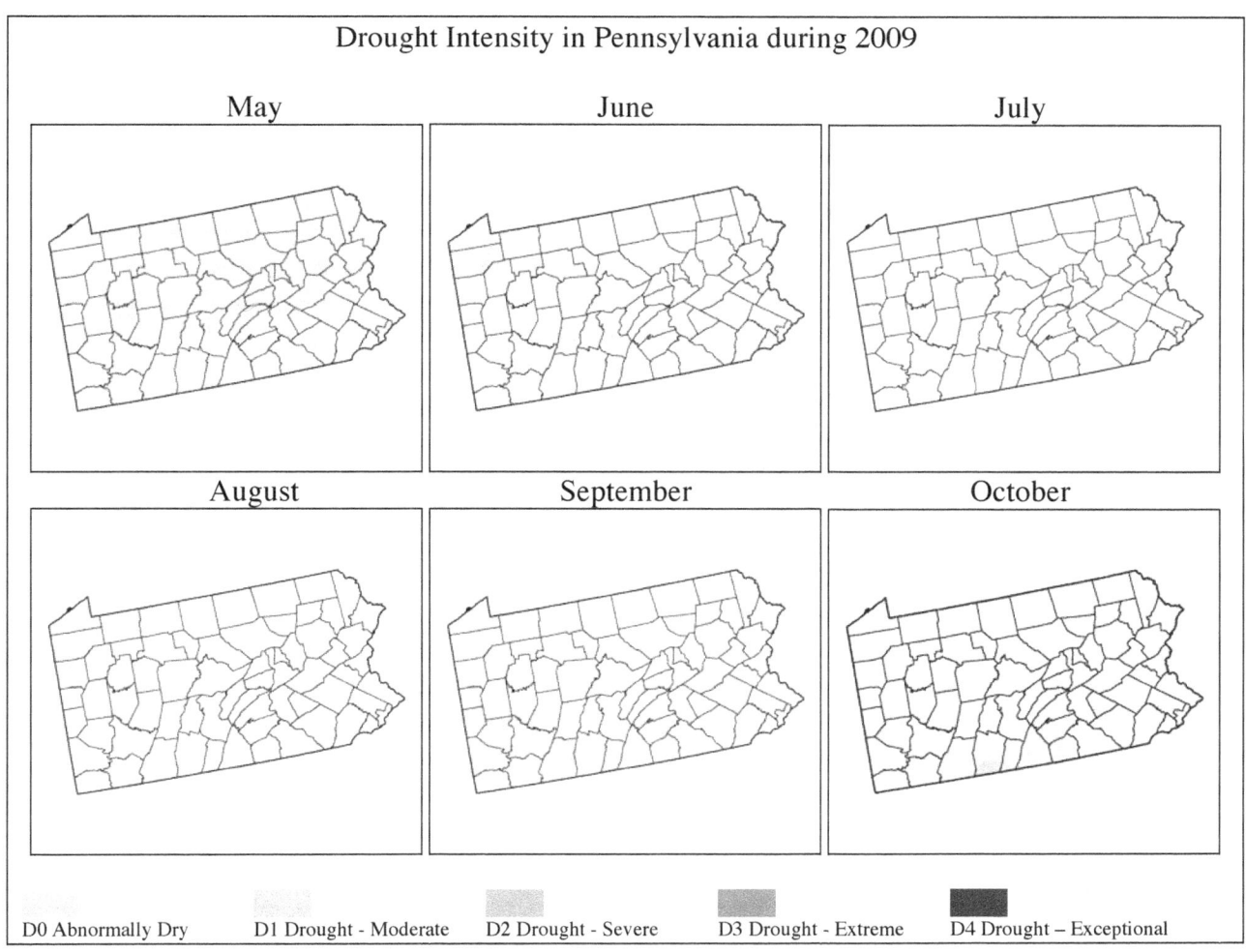

Figure 6. Mid-month values of the Drought Monitor - Drought Intensity Index for Pennsylvania in 2009.

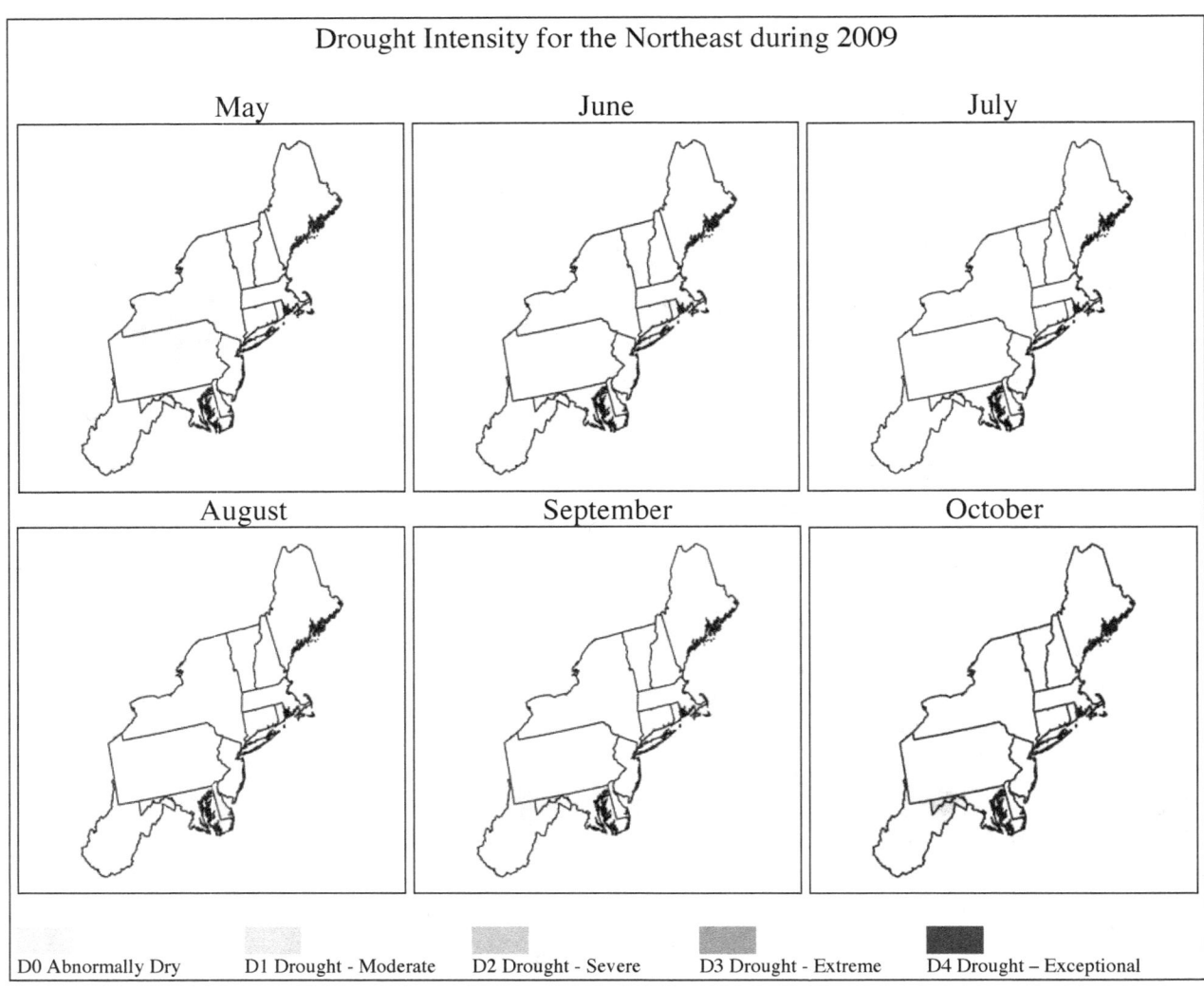

Figure 7. Mid-month values of the Drought Monitor - Drought Intensity Index for the Northeast in 2009.

References

Bureau of Land Management. 1997. Remote Automatic Weather Station (RAWS) and Remote Environmental Monitoring Systems (REMS) standards. RAWS/REMS Support Facility. Boise, ID.

Daly, C., W. P. Gibson, G.H. Taylor, G. L. Johnson, and P. Pasteris. 2002. A knowledge-based approach to the statistical mapping of climate. Climate Research 22:99-113.

Gelber, B. 2002. The Pennsylvania Weather Book. Rutgers University Press. New Brunswick, NJ.

Knight, P., T. Wisniewski, C. Bahrmann, and S. Miller. In preparation. Weather and Climate Monitoring Protocol for the Eastern Rivers and Mountains and Mid-Atlantic Networks. Natural Resource Report Series NPS/ERMN/NRR—2010/###. National Park Service. Fort Collins, CO.

Kocin, P. J., and L. W. Uccellini. 2004. Northeast Snowstorms Volume 1: Overview. Meteorological Monographs. Vol 32. No 54. American Meteorological Society. Boston, MA.

Marshall, M. R., and N. B. Piekielek. 2007. Eastern Rivers and Mountains Network Ecological Monitoring Plan. Natural Resource Report NPS/ERMN/NRR—2007/017. National Park Service. Fort Collins, CO.

National Assessment Synthesis Team. 2001. Climate Change Impacts on United States: The Potential Consequences of Climate Variability and Change, Report for the U.S. Global Change Research Program. Cambridge University Press. Cambridge, UK.

National Oceanic and Atmospheric Administration (NOAA). 2008. National Climatic Data Center. Climate of 2008 – Annual Review, Global and U.S. Summary. http://lwf.ncdc.noaa.gov/oa/climate/research/2008/ann/us-summary.html.

The Department of the Interior protects and manages the nation's natural resources and cultural heritage; provides scientific and other information about those resources; and honors its special responsibilities to American Indians, Alaska Natives, and affiliated Island Communities.

NPS 423/105522, 439/105522, September 2010